Triumph Through Tragedy

Relying on God When Things Seem Hopeless

Rob Schmersal

TABLE OF CONTENTS

Introduction

Psalm 23:4

"⁴Yea, though I walk through the valley of
the shadow of death, I will fear no evil; For
You are with me; Your rod and Your staff,
they comfort me."

Psalm 55:22

"²²Cast your burden on the Lord, And He
shall sustain you; He shall never permit
the righteous to be moved."

An officer answered Luke's phone. He said, "Is this Luke's dad?" I said, "Yes." He said, "Your son has been in an accident." This is how the journey began, or did it?

Do you ever feel like a challenge is so great you cannot overcome it? Are you facing a medical challenge that is out of your control? Do you feel like you don't know which way to turn? Do you wonder if anything good can come from the current tragedy? We have all been there. These feelings are normal and they can serve a purpose. I am here to tell you it is not hopeless.

In this book, I am going to share with you our journey. We have had some of these situations in

1

our life. God has been very good to us. It has not been easy, but He prepared us. I will share with you what God has taught us through the trials of the last year and a half. I will show you how you can take these lessons and apply them to your life. If you use them, they will help you through your trials. My goal is to show you how God is always at work. In the good times and the bad, He is working all things for His plan if you turn to Him.

My wife, Anji, and I have five children. They range in age from nineteen to eight. Luke is our oldest. We have homeschooled all of them from the beginning. Anji is a stay-at-home wife and mother. I am an electrical engineer. We have always tried our best to live our lives intentionally for God.

I can't believe I am writing this book. I was not a good English student. I have never liked writing. I am not even an avid reader, but I have felt an urging to share our story with you. I know that if you apply the things in this book, your life will be changed. You will look at the trials in your life differently.

Others have written similar books. I believe this one is different. I am not going to claim to be a better author. What I will tell you is that this book is not about theory. I am not going to tell you stories about other people or stories that are made up to show application of God's word. The things in this book really happened. The emotions I will share are what we felt. We didn't always make the correct decisions, but we did our best to follow God's word. I will share with you how that helped us and the miracles that we witnessed along the way.

It has been a year and a half since the night of Luke's accident. It has been a journey. There have been so many experiences. We've experienced mountain tops, deep valleys, joy, pain, loss, and answered prayer. Any emotion I can think of, we have experienced in the last year and a half.

God is good. He will help you along the way if you invite him. He will bear your burdens, if you allow Him. As you read this book, I pray you will see a new way to Triumph through Tragedy. God will use the trials in your life to strengthen your faith as He has mine.

Come along with me on a journey. I will share with you our story. I will tell you how we prepared and how we endured. I will share the hard lessons we learned. I will show you how we triumphed in the tragedy. Don't go through another trial in your life without reading this book first.

Where it all began.

Hebrews 13:20-21

"20Now may the God of peace who brought
up our Lord Jesus from the dead, that
great Shepherd of the sheep, through the
blood of the everlasting covenant, 21make
you complete in every good work to do His
will, working in you what is well pleasing in
His sight, through Jesus Christ, to whom
be glory forever and ever. Amen."

John 16:33

"33These things I have spoken to you, that
in Me you may have peace. In the world
you will have tribulation; but be of good
cheer, I have overcome the world."

One of the things I have learned through this journey is that God prepares and equips us for the life He sets before us. We have to learn to listen and follow. I have not always been the best at that. Looking back, I realized how many times it took me to get it right. This journey is teaching me to be more obedient to God.

There is a song called "Glorious Unfolding" by Steven Curtis Chapman. It talks about trusting in God's promises. It tells how life in general does not end up how we had it planned, but how God has it planned. I will have to admit He does a better job than I do. In the moment, it is hard to see that. Looking back, it is amazing to see how He had it all worked out. I am going to share with you how God has worked in my family's life recently. I would not wish for anyone to go through what we have, but I would not give it back. We would not be the same people without the trials.

I am going to take you way back. This accident helped me to realize that this journey didn't start a year and a half ago. I am going to start when I was just a young man. I realize now that the Lord was ordering the steps then to get me to where I am now. I still made lots of dumb decisions and I didn't always follow His lead.

When I was about sixteen years old I started to pray that God would help me to find a girlfriend that would make a good wife. I can't say that I prayed this every day, but it was often. I had my ideas of who I thought would qualify. I shared those with Him. Not that He didn't already know what I was thinking. None of those panned out. Not even one date.

I was eighteen and disc jockeying for a dance at Ottawa Glandorf high school. That night I totally missed it. Looking back, there was a very nice young lady who was responsible for putting the dance together. She was trying to catch my eye. I was oblivious. I just wanted to get finished, tear down, and go see a band that was playing in the area.

I am an engineer. Technically I am pretty sharp. I learn technical things very quickly. You will probably figure out from my stories that I have been a slow-learner in areas that matter. Sometimes it takes God a few times to get through to me.

Over the next year, I dated a couple of girls. None seemed to be a good fit. It was about a year and a half after the dance, and I was going to the prom with my current girlfriend at the time. We were going with a group of her friends and their dates. One of the young ladies didn't have a date. She rode with my girlfriend and me. I now realize that she was the young lady from the dance. At the time, I was still oblivious.

My then girlfriend and I dated for a couple more months after the prom and broke up. We were not a good fit. About six months after this, I was out with some friends and we met some girls. We started hanging out together. One of the young ladies was the one from the dance and the prom. I started to get to know her and found we were so much alike. We had both become designated drivers for our friends and enjoyed hanging out.

One day I decided that I wanted to take her out on a date. It took a while to get up the nerve to ask her after I made that decision. She made excuses the first few times I asked her out, but she finally agreed. The rest is history. A few years later, Anji and I were married. God was answering my prayer; it just took me a few years to figure out that it was Anji whom He was sending my way.

It is amazing looking back how God ordered our lives. Before we were married, Anji and I met a couple that homeschooled their children. We decided, well Anji says I decided and convinced her, that if we had children, she would stay home and homeschool them. Anji had been told that she might not be able to have children. I am not sure why, but I always felt that the Lord would bless us with children. About a year into our marriage, we had a miscarriage. We didn't even know that Anji was pregnant. This was a happy and sad time all together. We were very happy to know that conception was possible, but the loss was very sad.

Anji was struggling with very debilitating migraines around this time. They would cause paralysis in one side of her body. We went to a lot of doctors trying to figure out what was going on and what we could do to make her better. It was not uncommon for one of these migraines to make her bedfast for several days. One of the local doctors prescribed several medications. These just seemed to mask the symptoms. We continued to search for answers. She was finally referred to a neurologist in Columbus, Ohio. After a few visits and some tests, he diagnosed her with Familial Hemiplegic Migraines. He asked us if we wanted to have children. We told him absolutely. Then he told us that the medication she was taking was keeping her from conceiving. That was an answer that we had been looking for. He prescribed several new medications. We spent the next several months adjusting her medications to see what worked best.

It was like Anji received new life. She was able to function again. A short time later, she was pregnant. I will never forget the day we found out. We were at Cedar Point riding roller coasters. After the third time that morning that Anji ran to the bathroom sick, it hit me. I said, "You're pregnant." We stopped on the way home and purchased a pregnancy test. It was positive! We were happy and scared at the same time.

Nine months later Luke was born. Shortly after he was born, Anji graduated from college. She was working for Crime Victims Services, and was writing a handbook for a Victim Ministry Volunteer program. They let her finish it from home. After that, she resigned and came home to raise Luke. It was hard at the time. The loss of income was tough. We didn't have a lot of support from those around us for this decision, but we felt strongly that it was what God wanted us to do. Looking back, it was the correct decision.

Luke was followed by four more wonderful children. They are Faith, Rebekah, Lydia and William. We also had several more miscarriages along the way. They were never easy, but we thank God for the wonderful children we have here on this earth.

We followed through on our plan to homeschool. It has been a journey. It is amazing how different each child is. I don't know how the teachers in the schools do it. No two of our children learn the same way or at the same rate. Homeschooling allows us to tailor their education to what suits them best. I give Anji all the credit for this. I try to help when I can, but I travel a lot for work.

Luke was in his senior year when the accident happened. He had actually finished all his high school requirements the year before and was working on a degree in computer science. He was most of the way through his freshman year of college. Fortunately, we didn't have to deal with his needing to finish school and take exams to graduate. Looking back, it is clear to me now how God was directing our lives. He was preparing us. I can see how I was not always quick to listen. I have definitely been a slow-learner at times, but He did not give up on me. I am learning to listen and obey better.

Takeaway:

- When you feel gentle nudging, listen and be obedient to God.
- God has a purpose and a plan. We need to listen and follow.

The Accident

James 1:2-4

"²My brethren, count it all joy when you fall
into various trials,³knowing that the testing
of your faith produces patience.⁴But let
patience have its perfect work, that you
may be perfect and complete, lacking
nothing."

This part of our story starts on Monday, April 18, 2016. Anji's dad, Mike, was having a Heart Ablation at Ross Heart Center. Partway through the procedure they came out and gathered us into a room. They told us something had gone wrong. They perforated his heart and the sack around it filled with blood. This squeezed the heart and caused cardiac arrest. This would be the start of a journey that God used to prepare us. When we were able to see Mike several hours later, he was in an induced coma and on a ventilator. He had IV's everywhere. He was hardly responsive at all. We sat with him that way for days.

In hindsight, this was preparing us for what we would experience with our son just a week later. This was a test of patience and faith that God would bring Mike through this. And He did.

At the same time both, of my parents were experiencing serious health concerns. They were going through tests and setting up treatment to restore their health. They are also both doing well today.

On Sunday, April 24, 2016, I took the children, except for Luke, to the hospital to see Mike. Anji was still in Columbus with her dad. The children and I left mid-afternoon for home. I talked to Luke on the way home. He had gone to church, had lunch with my parents, helped my dad split a load of wood, mowed the lawn, and was working on his car.

When we arrived home, Luke was working on his car. Luke is always working on his car. I hopped on the mower to finish up the lawn. Luke went over to play some video games with the neighbor. He came home later and told me he was going to Bluffton to meet a friend.

It was almost 11:00 PM and Luke was not home. It was odd that he was not back yet and I had not heard from him. I tried to call and text him with no response. I tried to call Anji at 11:30 and she didn't answer. God protected her and let her rest.

I tried to go to sleep and could not. This was odd, because I hardly ever have trouble going to sleep. I started to call him again a little before 12:00. At

11:57 an officer answered Luke's phone, a parent's worst nightmare. He told me Luke had been in an accident and was lying in a field unresponsive. He took my number and said he would call me and let me know where they were transporting him.

I woke up our oldest daughter, Faith, and told her what was going on. She told me she was going to wake up Rebekah, our middle child, to pray with her.

I went out to the Yukon to call Anji and wait for the call back from the officer. Anji was still in Columbus with her dad. The officer called and told me he was being transported to St. Rita's Hospital in Lima, Ohio. I left to meet them there. Anji called me after she woke her mom and they were on the way. I was initially upset with Luke. I was going through all the things that he probably did wrong to cause the accident. Anji reminded me to focus on truth. We didn't know what happened or why. She read scripture to her mom and I while we traveled.

I got to the hospital, but Luke had not arrived yet. They put me in a waiting room. Through all of this, I prayed and had a peace that he was going to be ok.

They came and told me that he was there and headed for a CT scan. After the CT scan, they let me see him.

He had a bad cut on his head and his hands were bloody. He would not respond to me. They told me that the initial look at the CT scan was clear. He did not have any broken bones and no internal bleeding. They told me it appeared that he had a nasty concussion.

Shortly after this Anji and her mom arrived at the hospital. We stood there in the ER with Luke. He was just lying there. All his vitals were good; he just simply would not respond. They prepped him by numbing the area around the wound, cleaning it, and putting in nine staples to close the cut on his head. He yelled "ouch" when they put the staples in. This was encouraging to us. We thought maybe he was going to wake up, but no luck.

The ER doctor told us again they thought he had a bad concussion and we would just have to wait for him to wake up. They moved him to ICU. We waited in the lobby while they got him moved and settled. When we got back to the room, he just looked like he was sleeping. He even scratched his nose. We were still waiting for him to wake up.

About 6:30 AM we started to call and text people to pray. The gravity of the situation still had not hit me. I talked to my boss. He told me, "You take care of Luke and we will take care of work." What a blessing.

When shift change happened, one of our good friends showed up in the room. She told us that she was not supposed to be working that day; she was in to cover for someone. When she went to the morning meeting, she was startled to see Luke's name on the board, and that she was assigned to him. She told them she could not be his nurse, but needed to go check on us. What a true friend. She was there for us. She helped us process decisions we needed to make. She made sure we were taking care of ourselves. She told us, "You need to eat. If you don't take care of yourselves, you cannot take care of him." Truly arranged by God.

By midmorning, there were 50-60 people in the ICU lobby. They were there to pray for Luke and to support us. They brought breakfast for us. The staff could not believe the number of people that were there. We could not believe this outpouring of God's body.

Late morning, they told us the neurologist would not see Luke because he was not an adult and the neurologist was not comfortable working on a pediatric patient. They recommended that we transfer him to Nationwide Children's Hospital in Columbus, Ohio.

Around 2:00 PM Monday they transferred him by Mobile ICU. His friends wondered if they might transfer him by helicopter. They thought Luke would be very disappointed if he got to ride in a helicopter and could not remember it. Anji rode with Luke in the Mobile ICU. My aunt drove me to Columbus because I had been awake all night and was in no shape to drive.

When I got to Luke's room at Children's Hospital and saw all the people caring for him, I realized this was more than a bad concussion.

I don't think I was counting it all joy, but I was definitely trusting that God would bring all of us through this. It is hard to describe, but I just had a peace about the situation. God's word is true.

Philippians 4:6-7

"[6]Be anxious for nothing, but in everything by prayer and supplication, with thanksgiving, let your requests be made known to God;[7]and the peace of God, which surpasses all understanding, will guard your hearts and minds through Christ Jesus."

The one thing we knew for sure, there were lots and lots of people praying for Luke.

The doctors told us they needed to do an EEG to check for seizure activity. It is common for patients with head injuries to experience seizures. To do this, they had to put about 30 probes on his head in very specific locations. This was not an easy feat. Though he was not conscious, he was moving and reacting to the pain. We had to try to hold him still. My dad and my brother were in the room with me and several nurses trying to accomplish this. At one point a nurse came in to help. She was very petite. I am not sure she could have weighed much over a hundred pounds. We asked her, "Are you sure? He is very strong." The nurse responded that she was very strong and she could handle it. She said she would take a leg and give someone a break. The next thing we knew, the nurse was making a sound like Oh! Oh! Oh! We looked over to see that Luke had lifted her up in the air with his leg. I think this was God's way to lighten a very hard situation.

They did the EEG overnight. Tuesday morning, the doctors told us the EEG seemed normal for his state. They were looking for seizure activity and they did not see anything unusual. Luke was developing a bad cough. The doctors thought perhaps Luke had aspirated while he lay unconscious in the field. They said they expected aspiration pneumonia in one of his lungs. This was scary given his state of unconsciousness. The neurologist and physical medicine doctor told us they thought he had DAI (Diffuse Axonal Injury). They encouraged us to stay off the Internet and they would inform us what we needed to know, as we needed to know it.

There was a time around shift change that both Anji and I were sitting in the Family Lobby outside of ICU. I don't remember why both of us were out there. It was seldom that both of us would leave the room at the same time. The nurse that was leaving for the day came out to talk to us and sat down with us. She started to thank us for allowing her to care for our son. She was young. I think it affected her that she and Luke were close to the same age. She asked if we were Christian. We told her yes. She said she could feel it when she walked into his room. She knew something was different. She asked if it would be ok to add him to her church prayer chain. Then she asked to pray for Luke and us. This was so moving for me. I had no doubt that God was in this. We never saw that nurse again. I have wanted to thank her. I have recently discovered her name was Olivia.

We will never know what exactly happened to cause the accident. There were no witnesses and Luke does not remember. There were no drugs or alcohol in his system. He was traveling home on a country road around 11:00 PM. It appears that something came into his lane. He swerved and went off the left side of the road and brushed a very large oak tree. He then came back across the road and off the right side. There was a large dirt embankment on that side. His car went airborne and proceeded to roll multiple times through the field. The car was destroyed except for the area of the driver's seat. The roof on the passenger's side was smashed. That is what he hit his head on. There is no doubt that God protected him. If you looked at the car, you would not believe that anyone lived through the accident.

A man came upon the car just before midnight and called 911. He was on his way home from work. He told us that he almost never drives that route. I am thankful that he did that night.

This experience taught me to rely on God. I experienced firsthand His peace that passes all understanding. It was amazing how at peace I felt after I prayed and gave it all to Him.

Takeaway:

- Prayer works. Don't be afraid to pray boldly.
- The Body of Christ is very important. Find a good church. Don't be afraid to share your burdens with others. They can pray and minister in the situation.

The Diagnosis

The doctors told us they thought Luke had Diffuse
Axonal Injury (DAI). We were told to stay off the
Internet and they would inform us of what we
needed to know as we needed to know it. They
would schedule an MRI of the brain to confirm.
We asked, "What does this mean? When will he
wake up?" We were told to expect it to be weeks
to months before we would hear from him. That
was hard to take. We just assumed the doctors
were wrong and Luke was going to wake up and
we would go home.

They took him for the MRI around 5:00 PM. We
met with the anesthesiologist while they were
prepping him for the MRI. She explained the
procedure to us. She told us they would have to

intubate him. She told us that after the procedure they would extubate him and wake him up. I told her that would be awesome if she could wake him up. That was exactly what we were looking for. We all laughed and she apologized.

It might seem strange that they would have to give him anesthesia when he was unconscious, but he needed to remain very still for the MRI, and he was having a lot of involuntary movement.

The doctors tried to prepare us for what came next. I thought I had prepared myself as well. None of that was true. They told us there was a possibility that Luke may come back to the room on a respirator. I looked through the doors and saw them wheeling him back to the room with a respirator connected. I thought I was going to melt into a puddle. I found a corner and pleaded with the Lord to give me strength. I wanted to be strong for my wife and Luke.

We had to wait a little while for them to get him settled before we could go back to the room. It was very hard entering that room. From our previous experience with Anji's dad, we knew how to read the machine. It was obvious that it was doing all the breathing for him. I felt like we had just taken a giant step backwards. They did breathing treatments on Luke every couple of hours that night. Around 9:00 PM his doctor came in and showed us the results of the MRI. She showed us the broken Axons in his brain. Being an engineer, I asked, "Can we count them and determine how long before he wakes up?" She told me, "It doesn't work that way." She confirmed it was Diffuse Axonal Injury (DAI). She told us we would talk more in morning rounds. I prayed all night for encouragement. Later I would find out that Anji was praying for the same thing.

Music has always been important to me. A song came to my mind as I was trying to fall asleep. I liked the message of the song. Now it was taking on a whole different meaning. It was "Just Be Held" by Casting Crowns. Prior to this day, the message I got from this song centered around the lyric:

> *"Your world's not falling apart,
> it's falling into place*
>
> *I'm on the throne, stop holding
> on and just be held."*

This resonated with me. There have been lots of times in my life where I have felt that things were coming apart. In hindsight, it was God rearranging things for the better. It reminded me to trust Him. To let go and let God.

That night as the song played in my head, it felt like they wrote it for me. From the very first verse:

"Hold it all together
Everybody needs you strong.
But life hits you out of nowhere
And barely leaves you holding
on.

And when you're tired of fighting
Chained by your control,
There's freedom in surrender.
Lay it down and let it go."

I felt like it was my job as the dad and husband to hold it all together. I needed to be there for my wife. I wanted to do anything possible to help my son. But the truth is, as the song says, those were demands I was putting on myself. They are not commands from God. He wants all of us to rely on him. Yes, I needed to be there for my wife and son, but not by my power, but by His.

If that wasn't enough, my mind went to the next verse:

"If your eyes are on the storm
You'll wonder if I love you still.
But if your eyes are on the cross
You'll know I always have and I
always will.

And not a tear is wasted.
In time, you'll understand.
I'm painting beauty with the

ashes.
Your life is in My hands."

Wow. "Keep your focus in the right place," I told myself. "I don't know what the purpose is here, but I know that God will use it for His glory. God is in control and I need to rely on Him. God is good. He sent his Son to die for each of us. To save us from ourselves. One way or another He was going to put this all back together."

The last verse is as follows:

> *"Lift your hands, lift your eyes*
> *In the storm is where you'll find*
> *Me.*
> *And where you are, I'll hold your*
> *heart.*
> *I'll hold your heart.*
> *Come to Me, find your rest*
> *In the arms of the God who*
> *won't let go."*

It reminded me to praise the Lord in all things. James 1:2-4 "[2]My brethren, count it all joy when you fall into various trials, [3]knowing that the testing of your faith produces patience. [4]But let patience have its perfect work, that you may be perfect and complete, lacking nothing." I have never been closer to God than in the storm. I can't tell you how many nights in the last year and a half I have sung this song in my head to calm my mind to go to sleep. I have thanked God for His word and this song many times.

Through the early morning, they were able to start backing off the settings on the respirator. They removed the respirator first thing Wednesday morning. He was breathing on his own. His cough even sounded better. That was a miraculous recovery from pneumonia. God is amazing. I thanked God for the encouragement. The truth is I had no idea what He had in store for the day.

Rounds were like something I have never experienced before. There was a team of doctors, and they encouraged us to be a part of the discussion. They openly debated about what was going on with Luke and the best path forward. It was very interesting to be a part of this. We were encouraged to ask questions and provide input.

Wednesday morning rounds with the team of doctors brought the delivery of the official diagnosis. Diffuse Axonal Injury. He had bilateral damage on both frontal and temporal lobes. The doctors reiterated weeks to months of unconsciousness. They reiterated for us to stay off the Internet. They told us they would tell us what we needed to know. The day before we took him home, I did some research on the Internet. I found out why they told us not to look. I read a study of twenty-five patients with DAI. The study broke them into three groups. Luke would fall into the middle group, having damage to more than one lobe of the brain, but no damage to the brain stem. The average time to awake status was twelve and a half days. Average time to full consciousness was three months. We learned that God is not bound by doctors or statistics. Luke started to respond to commands. Not all of the time, but he was definitely having periods where he was. At one point when Anji was getting ready to leave the room for a few minutes, she kissed Luke on the forehead and told him she loved him. She was almost to the door and he said, "I love you too, mom." He spent most of the day unconscious. God did give us glimpses of Luke, and lots of encouragement.

It became clear to us that Luke was experiencing sensory overload. He would open his eyes for a short time. He would talk a little bit, but never at the same time. He could not talk or listen and look at the same time. He told us he was having a hard time distinguishing whether touch was pain or pleasure. We found that holding his hand was comforting to him as long as no one else was touching him.

They needed to put in an NG tube to get him some nourishment. During the process, Luke said, "ouch" and pulled it out. Then he said, "Give me a minute and I will do it." The nurse didn't know what to think. She just looked at us. We said, "Let him try." She told him, "Slide it in until you feel it hit the back of your throat. Swallow and push it in." He did it. She had been a nurse for over thirty years and she has never seen or heard of someone putting in their own NG tube. Maybe this is the reason God gave Luke a strong will. Over the next couple of weeks, we would see this strong will on amazing display. I am glad that we never broke it. Believe me, there were times when I wanted to, and tried.

Today would be the first time we would hear this phrase from many doctors, "There is no medical explanation for his recovery." Sometimes it would be followed by, "I have seen his MRI." We would tell them, "You are seeing the power of prayer." There were a lot of people praying for Luke and our family. The Christian TV station that Luke worked for posted a prayer request on their Facebook page. It had over 10,000 likes. They told us they have never had traffic like that before. Today we learned that God is bigger than any medical diagnosis.

On Thursday, Luke started with some therapy in his room. They had him out of bed and walking a few steps. It was very hard to watch my son, who had been walking for sixteen years, struggling to take a few steps. With one therapist on each side, they had to tell him, "Pick up your right leg; now put it down." I was starting to realize we had a long road ahead. When he was awake, he told us he wanted to eat. He had to be cleared by speech therapy before he could have food.

The speech therapist came in to test Luke's ability to swallow, but he would not wake up. I knew he was going to be very disappointed. Fortunately for him she came back when he was awake later in the day. He passed. He was very happy. There was a lot of progress in the 45 minutes that Luke was awake that day.

He would leave ICU by the end of the day. He was still spending more time unconscious than awake. They explained to us that the times of unconsciousness were his brain healing. He ate his first food in the new room. It took a lot to get him to come to and decide what he wanted. He ordered quesadillas and stuffing. When his food came, we woke him, and he just looked at it. I told him to eat. He ate the quesadillas, and started to eat the stuffing with his hands. We told him there was a fork on the tray. He picked it up, then put it back down, and continued to eat with his hands. As soon as he was finished, he was back out again.

We spent some time talking to Dr. Rosenberg, the physical medicine doctor from rehab. He felt like Luke was ready for rehab as soon as the rest of the medical team would release him. He stressed that research had shown that, the earlier rehab is started, the better the results. He also told us no visitors. We needed to focus all of Luke's energy on healing. This was hard to take. The visitors were helping to keep us sane. We assumed that when we let people know that Luke could not have visitors, they would stop coming to see us as well. Thank the Lord they did not. People were very understanding. They brought me real pop; the hospital only had diet. They also brought us food, music, money, hugs, and a lot of prayers.

That night Luke spiked a high fever. He had been running a low-grade fever for a few days. No one was concerned about that. He was fighting an infection in his lung. He was also not able to urinate on his own. The doctors were very concerned about the high fever. They did a lot of tests overnight. The fever dropped into a safe range by morning. The X-ray of his lungs showed improvement.

In the morning, he was awake and ordered an omelet and French toast. They wanted to do an ultrasound of his kidneys and bladder. He was awake so they took him down in a wheel chair. He went back into a state of unconsciousness on the ultrasound table. We were not sure how we were going to get him back upstairs. We were finally able to wake him transfer him to the wheelchair. They reassured us that this waxing and waning was normal for DAI.

Luke was actually awake for five to six hours that day. He was assessed by physical therapy, occupational therapy, and speech therapy. They were forming a plan. At the end of the day, they came in and told us he was being released to move to Rehab. A new journey was beginning. Dr. Rosenberg told us, "He is crushing the time line." God is amazing.

Takeaway:

- God is not bound by doctors or a diagnosis.
- Don't lose hope.

Rehab

Romans 12:12

"12Be joyful in hope, patient in affliction, faithful in prayer."

Isaiah 40:29

"29He gives power to the weak, and to those who have no might He increases strength."

The two weeks in rehab were a whirlwind. His room number in rehab was forty-three. That was his basketball number. Coincidence maybe, but I don't think so. Several times the doctors would tell us he is "Crushing the time line." Our good friends had shirts printed with the phrase and the number forty-three. We continued to pray and thank God for the healing He had done and was doing in Luke. We thanked Him for the strength He was giving us.

When Luke moved to rehab, they told us he could wear his own clothes. Luke was beginning to wake up and we knew he would soon realize he was living in a hospital gown. Getting him into "real" clothes would be a good thing for him. They recommended sweat suits or workout clothes. People were continually asking how they could help, so we let them know of the need for clothing. Our oldest daughter, Faith, used one of the gift cards we had received to go shopping. She chose clothing she knew her brother would like.

My brother, Jeff, came to visit and brought some clothes to the hospital for Luke. Luke was very excited to receive them. It was a new Under Armor sweat suit. We asked him if he wanted to put it on, but he told us, "Not now." This seemed strange to us. We told him that he didn't have to stay in the hospital gown. We would soon figure out that he forgot what we told him about the clothing. We quickly learned that he forgot most everything that was new information. The doctors told us he was going to struggle with short-term memory for a while. He was acting sleepy; this was normal. He could not take much interaction. We decided to go to the family room to visit. Jeff and I headed down the hall and Anji went to the nurses' desk to let them know we were stepping out for a little bit. Luke could not be left alone. He needed a constant, someone watching him at all times. He was a fall risk and could not remember that he was not allowed out of bed on his own. The nurses' desk was very close to his room. We figured it was ok for him to be there for the minute or less it would take Anji to tell them. We thought he was sleeping. When Anji got back to the room and opened the door, Luke dove back into bed. His hospital gown and gate belt were lying on the floor at the end of the bed. He had the new clothes on. Anji asked him why he did that. She told him we would have helped him. He said, "I thought that I would have had to take them back off if I tried them on." This should have been a clue to us that his mental processing was not working well. It also showed us we could not leave him alone at all, not even for just a few seconds. We could not take the risk of his falling.

It was very hard to see our strong, physically-fit son struggle to walk, but he was very determined. When they told him he could stop getting blood thinner shots when he could walk two laps, he said, "Let's go." God had prepared Luke's body for this as well. His strong muscles helped him to bounce back physically very quickly.

A few days into therapy the physical therapist asked him if they could take a water break. We all got a chuckle out of that. She was having a hard time keeping up. He was discharged from physical therapy before the end of the two weeks. They told us it is not common to discharge a patient in rehab from physical therapy first, but he was doing well and they wanted to focus more time on the cognitive issues.

Sometime during the first couple of days, the occupational therapist took him to the ice cream counter in the therapy room. She asked him how much he thought an ice cream bar was. Luke said he thought seventy-five cents. She said, "There are four of us here. How much for four of them?" Luke said, "Three dollars." He was always very good at math. The therapist handed him a piece of paper and asked him to write the problem out. He tried it three times and got the wrong answer. Then he just crossed it out and wrote down three dollars. I almost started crying. I had to walk out of the room.

Rehab took up most of the eight-hour day. Luke had a couple of breaks. When he had a break, he would come back to the room and lie down. He was out almost immediately. It was very hard to wake him. The doctors told us that he was actually slipping back into the coma, but that this was good. It was when his brain was healing. We quickly learned that he was most responsive to my voice. I could wake him when no one else could. I never left his side for more than an hour during the three weeks he was in the hospital.

Luke was having trouble going to the bathroom. The doctors told us this was common for brain-injury patients. It only took a few days for his brain to figure out how to go again. The problem, though was that he could not feel when he needed to go. The nurses would do bladder scans to see how much urine he was holding. He had to be put on a schedule around the clock to go to the bathroom. Every couple of hours, day and night, we had to get him up to go. If he couldn't or wouldn't go, he would need a catheter again. The job of waking him up fell on me. He would not wake up for anyone else, and I was glad I could be there to help him.

Throughout rehab they continued to uncover deficiencies. They worked to help him re-teach his brain. The days in rehab were long. They kept him, and us, busy from 8:00 AM until 5:00

PM Monday through Friday, until noon on Saturday, and he got Sunday off. It was worth it, as we could see improvements every day.

Luke had lost a lot of weight the first week in the hospital. They told us it was important for him to eat and gain it back. All the activity of therapy gave him a healthy appetite. He began ordering his own food. Sometimes he called on the phone, other times he used the TV. There were a few things that were common to every order; he always ordered cheesecake for breakfast, lunch, and dinner. He usually ordered two main courses. Slowly he started to gain some weight back. He almost never shared his cheesecake with me. Luke also found out that there was a refrigerator and snack cupboard on the rehab floor that was open to patients and parents. We made frequent visits to both. In between therapy sessions, he would stop by for some ice cream before he fell asleep.

They did all kinds of activities in Rehab. They were split into physical therapy, occupational therapy, speech therapy, and recreational therapy. He also received daily massages. This was our first experience with therapy. It was intense. Anji and I attended most of the sessions with him. The therapists told us it was amazing how much quicker the patient recovers when they have family with them, but, unfortunately, it is not the norm. One therapist told us she often meets the parents for the first time at discharge. We were glad that God had led us to order our lives so we could be there during that time.

We learned a lot of new games in Rehab. A majority of them were focused on memory. The therapists were trying to help his brain reconnect the memory channels. We were challenged too! He was healing so fast. He soon became hard to beat, but it seemed like each day of forward progress uncovered something else that he could no longer do.

Luke had been helping on the pit crew for a dirt track stockcar race team. It was something he loved. He was fixated on getting back to the track. This made the doctors and us very nervous. One of the areas of Luke's brain that was damaged, the frontal lobe, helps a person discern risk. We all know that this part of the brain doesn't work well in most eighteen-year-old males. Luke's frontal lobe was damaged and he had no inhibition. The doctors were also concerned that the noise could cause seizures or, at best, sensory overload, both of which would be very bad for his recovery.

The doctors and therapists were working to get Luke ready to re-enter the world. Luke was no longer a fall hazard, so they suggested we take him out to dinner. They told us to choose a noisy place with a lot of stimulation. We went to Buffalo Wild Wings. It was a favorite of Luke's. He did well, but he was exhausted by the time we got back to the hospital, but no big problems.

Knowing all this, Trevor, Luke's recreational therapist, contacted a local drag racing track and scheduled a visit. It was the middle of the second week in rehab. Luke's rehab team agreed that it would be a good test. They would be able to be with him and see firsthand how he would react. We were a little nervous, but we all knew that we were not going to be able to keep Luke away from the race track when he was released, so this was a great plan. The trip to the drag strip went well. We were so thankful to the staff for going the extra mile to help Luke progress on this journey back to normal. They told Luke it would be ok for him to go to the track, but not to the pits. That did not go over well with him, but it was very important that we keep Luke's head safe. Even a minor impact to the head could be detrimental to him.

They regularly assessed Luke's progress. He was testing very well against the standards (the average person his age), even though he was far from his normal. The rehab team told us they would not be able to justify keeping him past the initial two weeks they had approved with the insurance company. This was scary to us. We were ready to go home, but we liked the controlled environment and safety that rehab provided. The intense schedule was helping Luke make very fast progress.

The closer it got to discharge day, the more scared we got. We were fortunate that Luke did not have any other injuries besides the brain injury. This also made some things harder. Luke did not understand why he could not do some things and did not have any physical impediments to stop him. We talked to the doctor and decided together that it might be a good idea to show him the MRI. That didn't work so well. Luke's reaction was, "That doesn't seem so bad. Could have been a lot worse. Only two of four lobes were affected." While that was true, it was not what we were hoping for.

This experience made me a firm believer in rehabilitation. It amazed me the progress that focused effort brought. They worked to find ways to challenge him. They found activities that would help him get back to "normal" life when he went home. The Children's Rehab team was amazing! They were unbelievably focused and life-changing.

They helped us coordinate outpatient rehab that was close to home. He would leave the hospital with orders for Occupational Therapy and Speech Therapy. On our first visit to the therapy clinic, we were informed that the insurance company had denied to cover Speech Therapy. In our opinion, and the doctors', this is what he needed the most. Speech therapists help with cognitive skills, and his processing was still very slow. Even though Luke had made amazing progress, we were learning that this was going to be a journey.

Takeaway:

- Perseverance. Never give up no matter how hard it gets.
- Focus on the goal. When Luke decided that he didn't want the shots anymore, he was determined to walk no matter how hard it was.

Our Financial Journey

Psalm 24:1

"¹The earth is the Lord's, and all its fullness."

Proverbs 22:7

"⁷The rich rules over the poor, And the borrower is servant to the lender."

God prepared us financially for this journey. We were not fast learners. This was definitely not something that happened overnight. It took us a lot of years to get it right. It started shortly after Luke was born in 1998. We realized that we could not spend more than we were making. Congress still hasn't figured that out. Anji started researching finances. She found ways for us to live more frugally. Anji quit her job to be a stay-at-home mom when Luke was born. She made our finances and frugal living her new job. She read everything she could get her hands on. Some of it scared me. I drew the line when she started talking about separating two-ply toilet paper. We formed our first budget. We started to pay off some of our debt. We had credit cards, student loans, and a car loan.

We were currently renting a house. My dad was an outside salesman for a lumber company. He was telling us about a house one of his contractors was building that he thought would be great for us. He pointed out that house payments would be less than our rent. We started thinking about building a house, so we went and looked at the house he told us about. With a few changes, the house seemed perfect for us. We went to the bank to get some information. We were told that we could buy a house with little money down, but we needed 15% down if we were thinking about building. We didn't have that much money.

We were praying for God's guidance regarding a house. We considered buying one that we could remodel, but I did not want to do that. A few months later, I was sent to Margarita Island, Venezuela, for work. I could see that this was going to be a long-term project. After the first week, I told the owner of my company that I would stay if the company would fly Anji and Luke there. They arrived after I had been there three weeks. The three of us lived there in a hotel for three and a half months. It was one of the best things that could have happened to our marriage. God knew it was just what we needed. I worked lots of hours there, but without other distractions, we grew very close together.

When we arrived home, we checked our bank account. That was back in the days before instant Internet banking. We were amazed. In our account was the down payment for the house we wanted to build. God is amazing. It was clear to us that He wanted us to build a home. Now the search for land began. We looked at a lot of property. It was all too expensive or had restrictions that we could not live with. Our fallback was to purchase land from my grandfather. At the time, we saw this as a last resort. We were not sure that we wanted to live that close to family. In the end, we bought land from Grandpa. I thank God for closing all the other doors. Living next to my uncle and on the other side of the woods from my parents has been such a huge blessing.

A few months later we broke ground. My dad and I did the majority of the construction work. We had a very tight budget. It was amazing how God provided along the way. We wanted to upgrade the trim and doors from pine to oak. We prayed about this. God provided overtime money to pay for it. Construction was going well, but things were starting to get busier at work. I was having to travel more for my job. Anji and I were praying about the finishing of the woodwork. We were trying to figure out how we were going to get it done and not hold up the schedule. I had a job in

St Louis. Anji and Luke came with me. We arrived home after a couple of weeks. My dad handed us a quote for the finishing of the woodwork. He did not know that we were praying about this. He didn't even know we were considering hiring someone to do it. The amount of the quote matched to the dollar the amount of my overtime check. If this wasn't an answer from God, I don't know what would have been. Shortly after we moved in, I received a large raise at work. I am so glad for the timing. Had it come sooner, we probably would have built a larger house. Our house is the perfect size for our family.

Around 2002, our church was holding a Crown Ministries Bible Study. We decided to attend. The Bible references money and possessions more than 2,350 times. We learned that God owns it all. "The earth is the Lord's, and all its fullness"(Psalm 24:1) and that "The rich rules over the poor, And the borrower is servant to the lender." (Proverbs 22:7) I decided that it only applied to unsecured debt. We worked to pay off all the debt we had that was unsecured. We stopped using our credit cards. We still borrowed money for vehicles and we had a mortgage on our home. We put some money in an emergency fund. Within the next year, the company I worked for had financial trouble. Our paychecks were often late. Before we took the Crown course we had very little savings. We lived paycheck to paycheck. Had we not made this change, we would not have been able to pay our bills on time.

Fast forward to September 2011. Anji was feeling the Lord tell us we need to get rid of all of our debt. She saw the Financial Peace home study advertised on one of the homeschool buying sites. She recommended that we purchase it, and I agreed. I wasn't sure what we were getting into. Anji and I started to go through the study. The information was making sense to me. I was still not sure we could do it. In October 2011, I had to go to Nashville for work and brought the family along. On our way home, Anji asked if we could visit Financial Peace Plaza. While there, she showed me a spread sheet. It was a plan for us to pay off everything, including our home, in thirty months. We agreed to do it. We took a picture by the sign before we left. We talked to our children about our decision. We decided to set a reward of a large family trip to an all-inclusive resort in Jamaica. It was not easy, but we did it. It took us thirty- four months, but in July 2014, we were debt free. We built up an emergency fund of three to six months of expenses. I had heard people talk about the freedom of being debt-free. I had dreamed about it, but I had no idea how it would feel. When Anji and I sat down and realized that with no debt we could pay our bills on a very small income, it was very freeing. We did not have to worry about what we would do in the case of a job loss. Little did we know that the Lord was preparing us for what was coming.

When Anji's dad, Mike, went into the hospital, we needed to spend a week in a hotel. We did not worry how we were going to pay for it. We had saved up for a rainy day, and it was raining. I was so glad that we had followed God's prompting to pay everything off. We could focus on Mike's recovery and not on the money we were having to spend to be there. Being debt free creates a peace that I cannot describe.

Luke's accident happened while Mike was still in the hospital. I never thought for a minute what this was going to cost. Or how we were going to pay for this. I knew that all of our focus could be on Luke. It was during our second week in Columbus, when someone showed up at the hospital with a card from the Christian TV station where Luke worked. There was a pile of gift cards in that card; hundreds of dollars' worth. Our initial reaction was, "We cannot accept this." We have always been givers. God commands us to give. It feels good to give. We have never been good receivers. I think the initial reaction for me was pride. We had worked hard to be where we were financially, and we could do this on our own. We were wrong.

On our own financially was not God's plan. Day after day, friends would come to visit. They brought bags of food, snacks, gift cards, and money. A lot of it, we have no idea where or who it came from. I was handed envelopes of cash with the explanation of "I was asked to give this to you. You don't need to know where it is from." Or "God told us to do this and we are going to listen to Him, not you."

God was showing us that He was bigger than all of this. It definitely gave me a new insight on the power of giving. I knew that God wanted us to give, and it always felt good to do so, so we did. After this experience, I know why he wants us to give. It is an expression of His love. It is impossible for me to describe the feeling we received from these gifts. It has made me more in tune with other's needs. I now do a better job of recognizing where we can be a blessing to someone, even if it appears they are not in need.

My favorite thing is "random acts of giving." It is fun to pay for the person in the car behind you in the drive-through. I have a few of these memories that I will never forget. First I am going to tell you about one where I did not give. I was in line at Walmart in Findlay, OH. There was a young couple in line in front of me. They were checking out and their debit card was declined. They started to fight between themselves. Their groceries were nothing extravagant. I don't remember the exact amount, but I believe it was less than $100. God was prompting me to pay for it. I was concerned whether we had that much extra in our checking account. I knew we had money in savings, but I didn't want to risk the embarrassment of having my card declined too. The couple walked out without their food. I will never ever forget that day. I went out to the car. I told Anji, "I never want to be in that position again." I know without a doubt that God was telling me to pay for it, but I didn't trust Him. We were not where He wanted us to be financially. This is before we were debt-free. There is another time equally etched in my mind. William and I were in the Wendy's drive-through in Findlay, OH. I looked in my rearview mirror. There was a dad and three children in the car behind me. The young boy in the passenger's seat clearly had cancer. I felt it again. God telling me to pay for their food. I started to battle inside. Do I have enough cash? I decided, "I don't care. I will use the debit card if I have to." I was not going to make that mistake again. After I paid for our food, I asked, "How much is the next order?" It was less than $10. I wondered after driving away if the dad had ordered food for himself. God had blessed him that day through me. He had me there at that place and time for His purpose. And to think, I drove past the other Wendy's because I thought the line was too long.

One day in March, 2017, I received a call asking me to meet my supervisor's counterpart at 7:00 AM the next morning. My supervisor had become unavailable the week before with some untold emergency. This all seemed strange and I was pretty sure I was losing my job. I called Anji and told her that I was going to lose my job the next morning. She asked a few questions and I explained to her why I thought so. Anji told me, "Don't worry we will be fine." She was right. We had an emergency fund for just a time like this. The next morning, I went to the meeting and was told that my position was being eliminated. I no longer had a job. Driving away that morning, I was glad that I always did my best to put my family before my job. They truly were most important and what would last in my life. I was not stressed or worried about paying the bills. I actually felt relief. I had recently been under a lot of stress in the position I was in. I prayed to God for guidance and direction for where He wanted me. I reached out to a few people that night. I had a job offer before I went to bed. I took a few days and entertained some other possibilities. On Friday, I accepted a position with another division of the company I had been working for.

Day after day I am so glad that we listened to God and his word about money management. The scripture is so true. "The rich rules over the poor, And the borrower is servant to the lender." (Proverbs 22:7) When we were in debt, it was hard to follow God's commands to give. We had already promised our money to someone else. When we got our attitude right and realized that we were just managing God's money, things started to change. I can't even imagine how much harder these trials would have been with the added stress of money. The reality is, I can still remember when a car repair felt like a tragedy, and I don't ever want to go back there.

Takeaway:

- Debt is not God's plan.
- Prepare for a rainy day.

Rebekah

Rebekah is our middle child. She was 13 years old. It was Saturday September 3, 2016. It was Labor Day weekend. We were at a Christian equestrian camp. They were hosting a family work weekend and we were volunteering our time. My children and I were working in the firewood crew. Rebekah was helping run the log splitter. She got her arm caught in a splitter. William, our youngest son, ran to me and told me that Rebekah was hurt. When I went over to her, they had her arm wrapped in a towel. I could tell it was bloody, but I could not see how badly it was hurt.

Rebekah and I got into a truck so someone could drive us down the hill. We got in our vehicle and went to find Anji who was working in the kitchen. We left to go to the nearest hospital. We did not know the extent of her injury, but did not want to take the towel off to see. It was only a ten-minute drive to the hospital. Upon arriving, we went to the emergency room and registered. We had to wait for nearly a half an hour to be seen. We were starting to get very concerned. We knew she had an open wound and it needed attention.

They finally brought her back and unwrapped it. The whole top of her forearm was split completely open. It looked awful. Rebekah did not look at it. She did not want to. The nurse put a wet sterile dressing on the wound. We waited for the doctor to come and check it out. He came in and looked at it. He told us that it was a bad flesh wound. He said they would do a local and clean it and sew it up. Rebekah told him that her hand hurt and she couldn't move her fingers. We asked about doing a neuro exam and were told that he would do that when it was closed up. He told us that she needed to have a tetanus shot and we agreed. He numbed the area and the nurse came in and cleaned up the wound. We waited for the doctor to come back in and stitch her arm.

The doctor came back in to close up the wound. We asked again about the hand pain and the need to make sure everything was working correctly before closing it up. Again, he told us that he would check everything when he was done closing it up. He asked Rebekah if she wanted to see it. He told her it looked cool. She gave an emphatic "No." He kept pushing. He started to sew it shut. He put a stich in the middle. He told her it looked like a bow and that she should look. She said "No" again. I told him to quit. He finished closing it up. We reminded him to do a neuro check. He told Rebekah to wiggle her fingers. Then he told her to raise her thumb. He said, "Looks like you are good to go." Rebekah told him that her thumb was not working right. He said, "What do you mean?" She told him that her thumb would not go up at all. The doctor told her to try harder. He was really testing my patience. Then the doctor said, "Oh Crap. She needs to see a trauma team." We suggested Nationwide Children's Hospital in Columbus, OH, since we had experience there. The doctor agreed and started the paperwork to transfer Rebekah there.

The doctor said she needed to have the tetanus shot before she was transferred. After waiting another half hour to get the shot, I was getting very frustrated. My patience was running out. My daughter needed real medical attention and I was going to get it for her.

We left and took Rebekah to Nationwide Children's Hospital. We brought her straight to the Emergency room there. They were expecting her. She was taken right to a room. They asked us what happened. We explained everything. They asked if we brought the films. We told them they did not take an x-ray. Then they said, "Let's unwrap it and take a look." We told them it was stitched up. Fortunately, we had taken some pictures of the wound and could show them. They could not believe it. They were flabbergasted by the care that we received at the local hospital.

They did an x-ray. Both bones were fractured. They explained how an open fracture can be deadly. Infection can get straight into the bone. They immediately started Rebekah on three different IV antibiotics. It was just a minute or two and Rebekah said, "I feel itchy. My throat feels thick." She was breaking out in hives and having trouble breathing. She was reacting to the penicillin. The nurse immediately stopped the IV and called for help. There were several people there right away. They gave her some epinephrine to reverse the effects. Now we know that Rebekah is allergic to penicillin. She had never been on antibiotics before.

They did a full evaluation and told us she was going to need surgery to put things back together. They were going to admit her and continue with strong antibiotics. They would have to schedule the surgery as soon as possible. It would not be done as an emergency, because she was sewn up. It was Saturday of a holiday weekend. We hoped that we didn't have to wait until Tuesday. The ER staff was not making any promises.

In the morning, Dr. Somora, the surgeon, and her team came in. She explained to us what they were going to do. She told us it was very likely, based on the pictures, that the main nerve for the arm and hand was damaged. It runs along the top of the arm, and both bones were indented from the log splitter. She talked to us about the options to reconnect the nerve. We made what seemed like the best choices. They would take a nerve out of Rebekah's left leg and transplant it in her arm. They marked her leg for surgery. A few hours later they took Rebekah to prep her for surgery.

Surgery lasted about an hour. When it was over, Dr. Somora came out. She got out her phone and started to show us pictures. The first one was of the nerve. Not a bit of damage. She could not believe it. God protected the nerve. Then she told us that Rebekah had severed all seven extensor tendons in the top of her arm. These are what you use to lift your fingers and thumb. The damage was in the area where the tendons attach to the muscle. The doctor told us it is like attaching mashed potatoes to mashed potatoes. She said that they did their best. Rebekah would be immobilized in a cast for 6 weeks. Then we would start rehab and, in a year or so, they hoped she would have full use of her arm and hand again.

I asked about the elk hunting trip we had scheduled for October in Colorado. It was going to be Rebekah's first trip. She was looking forward to it almost as much as I was. We were told "Not this year." Then we asked about basketball. It was also the first year we were letting her play. The doctor told us that she would not be able to play this season. Then we asked about dance. Rebekah loved dance, and she was looking forward to getting her pointe shoes. It was her first year for pointe, and her shoes should be in soon. Again, we were told "No." Dr. Somora told us we couldn't let her do anything that would put the arm at risk. If she were to fall and hit her arm, it could pull things apart, and they would not be able to put it back together again.

We were so disappointed for Rebekah that she was not going to be able to do the things she had planned for that year. We were thankful that God had spared the nerve, and it sounded like she should gain full use of her arm again. We went up to the room to wait for them to bring Rebekah back. We were dreading having to tell her the bad news. We looked down the hall and saw her coming. She had a huge smile on her face. She said, "Look! They didn't have to take a nerve out of my leg to fix my arm!" She was counting it all joy. She told us the things she could not do were just temporary.

We had several appointments over the next six weeks. The bone was healing well. We started to talk about physical therapy. Dr. Somora recommended a hand specialist at the hospital. We decided that it was worth the two and a half hour drive each way if this was the best treatment she could get.

The day came. It was time to cut the cast off and start therapy. We were anxious. Therapy started slow. Lots of stretching and rubbing of the area to break up the scar tissue. They gave Rebekah exercises to do at home. She was very faithful. She did them just as they told her to. She was determined to get back to the things she loved. Anji massaged Rebekah's arm twice a day. This had to be painful for Rebekah, but she never complained. Twice a week Anji drove her to Columbus. The hours in the car turned into a special bonding time. I was able to go along a few times and really enjoyed this time with just Rebekah and Anji.

Rebekah chose to join the basketball team even though she could not play. We took her to every practice and game. She went to dance and sat in a chair. At some point she convinced Dr. Somora that it would be ok for her to do barre work in ballet, since she was holding on with little risk of falling. She was working very hard in and out of therapy. The therapist would set a goal for the next week. Rebekah would double or triple it. It was unbelievable the progress she was making.

At the beginning of January, we had a follow-up with Dr. Somora. She tested strengths and range of motion. She asked Rebekah to raise and lower each finger. Dr. Somora started to tear up. She told us that she never expected her to be able to move each finger by itself. She thought best case she would be able to lift them all together after a year of therapy. It had only been four months! This was a miracle. Dr. Somora asked if she could take some pictures. We agreed. Dr. Somora released her to play basketball and go back to dance. She encouraged her to do what she could, but not to overdo it. Dr. Somora asked us to send her some pictures of her playing basketball and dancing.

Rebekah was able to play in the last few regular-season games and the year-end tournament. It was clear that she was a little guarded, but she knew all the plays. She had been very attentive at practice, even though she was not able to be on the floor.

She started working very hard to rebuild her endurance for dance. She worked tirelessly at pointe. She even won a spot to be in a trio for the spring recital. I was so proud of her. Even with all the craziness going on with her brother, she remained positive and focused during this time. I saw her relationship with the Lord grow. She didn't get mad at God. She thanked Him for the healing.

I learned a lot from this trial. God taught me through Rebekah. He taught me to focus on the positive. When I was feeling down about what she was going to miss, she was praising the Lord for the good He had done. I learned that you need to always be a medical advocate for your children. The doctor is not always right. If we had not pushed at the first hospital, I am not sure where we would be today. God definitely used this as a distraction to the things going on with Luke. They were getting very bad at this time. This gave us something positive to focus on. God definitely used this tragedy for good. He always does. Most of the time we have to focus hard to see how.

Takeaway:

- Focus on the blessings.
- God will use all things for good.

Coming Home

2 Corinthians 1:3-4

"³Blessed be the God and Father of our Lord Jesus Christ, the Father of mercies and God of all comfort, ⁴who comforts us in all our tribulation, that we may be able to comfort those who are in any trouble, with the comfort with which we ourselves are comforted by God."

Exodus 14:14

"¹⁴The Lord will fight for you, you need only be still."

Discharge day was one of the happiest and scariest days of our lives. We were realizing how blessed we were to be taking Luke home in the condition he was. He was so far ahead of where anyone expected him to be, but far from well. They told us a lot of scary things to watch for and expect. Unfortunately, they were spot on. They told us to expect him to take one to two years to wake completely and another five to seven years to continue to heal. There is truly no way they could have prepared us. We have trusted in the Lord to help us through, and He has been faithful.

When we got home, we were not sure what to do. They told us we needed to watch him at all times. Due to the area of his brain that was damaged, the frontal and temporal lobes, he had very little filter or inhibition. In the past, we did lots of stuff together, but he became quickly annoyed with me following him around. He could not drive and that was to our advantage. He wasn't able to go far without us.

They told us at the hospital that it was great that he wasn't hurt physically, but this was going to make going home difficult. Luke would not understand that he had limitations. He was not allowed to do anything that took his feet off the ground; no bicycle, no sports, and no pit crew.

My dad and I took Luke to the races the first night home. We sat in the stands. He was not very happy about this. He wanted to be in the pits where the action was. I explained to him this was just temporary. Some of his friends found out that he was going and showed up. Things went well at the track. It was an emotional night for many people.

To people who did not know Luke well, and even to some who did, he seemed fine. This made things hard. Some would say, "Let him go." They did not understand that Luke really no longer had a healthy fear. He would not survive another head trauma.

Luke started outpatient rehab near home. The first day we arrived, they informed us that the insurance had approved occupational therapy, but not speech therapy. We could not believe this. Speech therapists work on much more than just talking and swallowing; they also deal with cognitive things. This is what he needed most.

After therapy, I called the insurance company. They told me it was not approved based on his diagnosis. I asked how they could possibly think that you would not need speech (cognitive) therapy for a traumatic brain injury. She explained it all works on codes. I would need the provider to resubmit the request. I called the local hospital that was providing the rehab. They told me that Luke's doctor at Children's would have to resubmit it. I called them. They could not understand what was going on. They worked with the insurance company to get them the documentation that they needed to justify the treatment. We reached out to people to pray about the outcome of this situation. About two weeks later, we received a letter in the mail that said he was approved for speech therapy. That was great news!

When the bills started to come in two or three months later, the insurance company refused to pay for the speech therapy. Again, I began making phone calls. I spent many more hours back and forth with them. Fortunately, I kept the letter. I reminded them each time I called that I had a letter in my hand that stated that it was approved based on the documentation that was submitted. There were several other crazy things I had to deal with regarding the insurance company. There were several things they paid and then revoked the payment from the provider. In these cases, the provider just billed us. It was a mess. I kept all the paperwork in a folder. It took a lot of phone calls to get it all fixed. In the end, with a lot of prayer and persistence, everyone got paid what they were due and we didn't end up in collections.

By mid-June, Luke started back to work at the TV station as the floor director. It was just one or two days a week. We were all a little nervous about how it would go. The station personnel were great. The first day or two they had someone on standby in the wings. Luke never needed it. He remembered everything. They told us he went back into the same routine he always followed. Those who knew him well could tell something was different. His personality was off. He was flat and his eyes were disconnected; no spark in them. We had to drive him everywhere, but we didn't mind. We were glad to see some things getting back to normal.

Luke slept a lot. For several months, simple things would make him very tired. We are sure that he would slip back into an unconscious state. He would lie down and we could not wake him. The doctors told us to expect this. It was his brain healing. We started to just accept it. If he worked, had rehab, or did anything mentally taxing, he would be out for the day. We learned to encourage him to eat before lying down, because we knew he needed nourishment and he probably would not wake up again.

Our Homeschool group, delayed the graduation ceremony so that Luke could attend. We were thankful for that. We waited until the end of June to have a graduation party. The medical team told us we should wait 8 weeks after the accident if we wanted any possibility that he might remember. It was a great celebration of Luke's life. We were so grateful to still have him. A lot of people came to celebrate with us.

Luke quickly graduated out of rehab. They told us, even though he was not back to normal, he was above average and they could not justify more treatment at the center. He would need to continue therapy at home. This was another hard day. We could not get him to do the rehab activities at home. He didn't think anything was wrong; his frontal and temporal lobes were damaged. When he tried some of the things they suggested, he found that he could not do them. He became discouraged, and he stopped.

At his follow-up appointment on July 22, 2016, they cleared him to drive. This was really scary. We knew that he was doing well. They were concerned that he would have seizures as the brain healed and, at this point, he hadn't had any that we were aware of. The first few times he left we were concerned that something would happen. The first weekend he was out with his friends he hit a deer on his way home. Fortunately, it was not bad and Luke was ok.

Anji was really struggling every time he left the house. We sat down and talked about it. We agreed that we had never parented with a spirit of fear. We were not going to start now. God had saved Luke's life. He protected Luke for a reason. God has a purpose and a plan for each of our lives. The reality was there was nothing we could do anyway. We had to trust God with Luke. Before the accident, we laid the children at the feet of Jesus where they belong. God entrusted the children to us to raise, but they are not ours; they belong to Him. And this included Luke. This is something we would have to remember daily over the next year.

In September, Luke started to talk about getting a full-time job. College was out of the question at this time. Prior to the accident, he was almost through his freshman year in Computer Science. He had been taking online classes since his junior year.

Luke shared with my parents that he did not know how to find a job. This was weird. He was very well spoken. We had never helped him get a job before. He had three part-time jobs before the accident. They helped him look in the newspaper to see what was in the area. He ended up getting hired at a local auto dealership in the service department. This meant that he had to quit the Christian TV station where he had worked for two years. We were concerned about his leaving there. They were a very positive influence on his life. A full-time job was probably a good thing for him. The doctors and therapists encouraged us to work on structure to encourage healing. He needed to fill his free time with something constructive.

At first, things seemed good with the new job. We soon found out that Luke purchased a toolbox from one of the guys there. He was making weekly payments. Then he bought tools from several of the tool trucks on credit. Before the accident, he would have never done this. The crazy part was that he was a service writer. He did not need tools to do his job. It became evident that he wanted to become a mechanic. He moved into the detail department. He worked there for a while. In December, they let him go. This was all so difficult for us. We would try to compare the "new" Luke to the Luke before the accident. The previous places of employment raved about what a hard worker Luke was and what a great manner and work ethic he had.

The day Luke was let go, he came home, changed his clothes, and told Faith not to tell us he was there. He wanted to find another job before we found out. He went to the dealership that my dad retired from as a salesman. He asked my dad who to talk to. Luke interviewed with them. They asked him if God told him to come there. They had posted a job that morning. They decided that they wanted to hire someone local, and not a tech student. He started the next morning. He called and told us after he had the job. We were proud he had persevered.

In January 2017, we were in Tennessee. I had work meetings there and the family had come along. Luke and Faith stayed home to work. We got a call early one morning. Luke had wrecked his car on the way to work. He hit a pole and totaled his car, but, fortunately, Luke was ok.

Luke was starting to pull away more and more. He was no longer coming home every night. Luke was no longer going to church. Before the accident, his faith was strong. He would go to church by himself if the rest of us were out of town. He did on the day of his accident.

Through all of this we relied heavily on counsel. We had another Christian couple who we met and prayed with regularly. We also met with our pastor. Our goal was to make sure we represented God well. In situations like this, it is easy to let emotion carry you away. Having mentors kept us grounded in God's word. They helped us see things from a different perspective.

We learned to cover everything in prayer. When things would get really tough, we would reach out and ask people to pray for us and the situation. Some would say, "You need to do more than pray." We knew that prayer was the best thing we could do. Exodus 14:14 "The Lord will fight for you, you need only be still." We saw the Lord answer in ways we never dreamed of. Through it all, we learned to pray and get out of the way. We still meet people that ask us, "How is Luke?" Then they tell us that they pray for him every day.

In February, Anji and I went to Florida for a long weekend. Luke was taking care of Mom and Dad's wood furnace. He was staying at their house. We came home to find that he had let the furnace burn out several times. He also had a party at their house. It was a mess. We confronted him about it and it got pretty ugly. He was pulling away from us and the morals and beliefs that he had prior to the accident.

When my parents arrived home from Florida, they told him he could stay for a couple of weeks as long as he followed some basic rules. They thought this would help him straighten some things out and then come back home. One of the basic rules was that he had to let them know when he would be there.

On a Friday night, Luke called and asked if he could take Rebekah to breakfast before her tournament game. We struggled with this decision. We had not let any of our children ride with him since the accident. We went back and forth. We finally decided it would be ok. We let him ask her. They agreed on a time: 6:45 AM.

Saturday morning came. Rebekah got up and got ready, but Luke never showed up. We tried to call him. He didn't answer. We were ready and left to take Rebekah to the tournament. Luke showed up at the tournament about 10:00 AM. He looked very rough and our hearts were heavy for him. He had been at a party and was in a fight.

My dad told him that day he needed to leave their house. He had broken the rules. He came back home, but we saw him less and less. We told him there are basic rules that he must follow at our house and he needed to be respectful, because we love him and all of our children. We found that he was only coming to the house when he knew we weren't going to be there. Anji stopped coming to church on Wednesday nights. He would show up at the house just after we left and be gone when we got back home.

It was the first weekend in May. We were out of town for the weekend. We came home to find evidence that he had broken the rules while we were gone. We took the garage door opener from Luke. He had already lost his house key. We let him know that he was only welcome at our home when we were there.

I had to leave for Texas early the next morning. I felt really bad leaving Anji in this situation. We were sure we would never hear from him again. What happened next was a God thing. We had covered all this in prayer and God answered. By the middle of the next morning, Luke was reaching out to us. He was reeling. He was calling and texting constantly. I was in a meeting and could not respond immediately. He was not angry, which is what we expected. Later that day, I was able to call him and we were able to have real conversations about what was going on. He told me that he felt like his family didn't like him. I helped him understand how he had abandoned his family. I told him that it was going to take time for him to earn people's trust again. We agreed that open communication was key.

I talked to Luke almost every morning on his way to work. No matter where I was, I would get up early, if I had to, to call him. This was not always easy. Some mornings he would just say hi and hang up. Some mornings we would have a real conversation. After a couple of days in a row of nasty words and a hang-up, I wanted to quit calling. Anji always encouraged me to continue. He would not talk to her at all. All she ever got from him was nasty.

We did our best to show him God's love. We tried to take Luke out to dinner once a week. During this time, we just loved him. We didn't badger him about the things he was doing wrong. We knew that deep down he knew. I kept calling no matter how hard it was. He came home occasionally. He seemed to respect our rules when he was here.

On June 1, Luke was let go from his job at the dealership. He called Anji and said, "Mom, I want to come home." She told him that was great, but the problem was that Anji and the children were on their way out of state to meet some old friends for a few days, and I was in Texas again for work. He spent a couple of nights with my parents.

He started looking for a job right away. My parents called and asked me if they could pay him for some work they needed done. I told them it was fine as long as he worked for the money. Luke called my uncle that does contracting work. He said he could use him a few days the next week. Luke worked for him for a couple of weeks.

Luke had always had a dream of going to Texas. He was there when he was young, but he didn't remember it. I offered to take him for a long weekend. I thought this would be an opportunity for us to reconnect and talk. He agreed and was very excited to go. We scheduled it for Father's Day weekend. We flew into Dallas and rented a convertible. We drove to San Antonio and saw the Alamo. Through the weekend, I saw a lot of the old Luke. We had a lot of fun. We ate some good food. Luke and I both really liked BBQ. We capped the weekend off with a round of sporting clays. I lost. I felt like we rebuilt some bridges.

Another one of my uncles told me they had an opening in the factory where he worked. We talked about it, and it seemed like it might be a good fit. I asked him to talk to Luke directly. I thought he might respond better to him. I had asked Luke about another factory in the area and he told me he would not work there. We prayed that this would work out.

Luke responded well. He went and filled out an application. They called him for an interview and offered him a job on the spot. He started the new job June 19, right after our trip to Texas. He is still working there. Most days he likes it. His job is a good mix of technical work and physical work.

Through this time, we could see Luke changing. His attitude was better. He was treating people more kindly at home. This was a huge change. He was spending time with my parents again. He spent almost every night at home. He was happier in general. We were just thanking God for the work He was doing.

Our church does a God and Country night on the 3rd of July. Voices of Faith, a singing group from our church, sings some patriotic songs and we put on a firework display. Luke has helped me do sound for Voices of Faith for eight years. I asked him to help me again this year, although I didn't expect him to. I just prayed he would, and he agreed.

On July 1, we were at a family campout at my parents' house. We had a huge altercation with Luke. He was doing things that he knew he should not be doing. He left and told us we would never see him again. It was another hard night, but we knew we had to remain on the side of what was right.

We didn't hear anything from him the rest of the weekend. He would not answer our calls. We just kept praying for him. On the morning of July 3, I called him. I didn't expect him to answer, but he did. I asked him what time he would be at church to help me. He said early afternoon. I said OK and hung up. I could not believe it. I called Anji. I was almost in tears. I thanked her for encouraging me to call him. To God be the Glory!

That day, Luke asked if he helped me last year. I told him that he had. He shared with me that he did not remember most of the last year. He said that he knew he had done some bad things. He could see that all his friends were gone, but he was not sure what all he had done. I thanked him for sharing with me. I told him that we would get through this.

On Friday, August 25, 2017, Luke bought a motorcycle. This was very scary for us. Before he purchased the motorcycle, he bought a new helmet, gloves, and a riding jacket. I was proud of him for that and I told him so. On Sunday, August 27, he wrecked the motorcycle. He had a few scratches and scrapes, and his shoulder hurt pretty bad. He did not want to go to the emergency room. We let him try to rest.

Monday morning he woke up in a lot of pain and had to call into work to tell them he would not be in. He went to the chiropractor and they ordered an x-ray. Luke found out that his collar bone was broken and he would have to be off of work for 6 weeks. He was really worried. He had insurance bills and tool payments to make, and he had just spent all his money on the motorcycle.

The doctor told him to go see the HR manager and get FMLA paperwork. He told Luke that they would help him fill it out. Luke went to see HR. They told him that he was not eligible for benefits until that Friday. She told him that she would see what she could do. On Thursday, she called him and said they were going to pay him disability. What an answer to prayer!

Luke has continued to heal. Things at home get better all the time. In October, he wrote a letter to Rebekah apologizing for the day of her tournament that he didn't show up. He asked for forgiveness and expressed his desire to rebuild their relationship. Luke started going to the YMCA to play basketball with Rebekah. He engages in conversations and is very much a part of family life at home, including some Sunday morning breakfasts and family meals. We are rebuilding. We have been told of other accounts of his apologies to people. He has started to go to church again with a friend once in a while. He is still not consistent. He came back to our church to see the children's Christmas program this year and attended with us on Christmas Eve. It was great to have our family together in church again. We worshiped and even took a family photo. I am not sure there could have been a better Christmas present.

It has been a journey. It is not over. We continue to thank God and praise Him. We pray daily for Him to continue to work in our lives.

Takeaway:

- Pray and God will fight the fight.
- Cover it all with Love. That is the example that Jesus set for us.

Why Us?

Exodus 33:18

"Show me your glory."

Why Us? That could have lots of meanings. Some might ask, "Why did God allow these tragedies to happen to us?" I think a better question is, "How is God working in this seemingly bad situation?" The real question I have is, "Why did God choose us to witness His Majesty and Power first hand?" "Show me your glory." (Exodus 33:18.) Moses asked God to show him. Unlike Moses, we didn't ask God, but He has shown us loud and clear. I read a scripture that I think may answer part of the question.

Mark 4:36-41

"³⁶Now when they had left the multitude, they took Him along in the boat as He was. And other little boats were also with Him. ³⁷And a great windstorm arose, and the waves beat into the boat, so that it was already filling. ³⁸But He was in the stern, asleep on a pillow. And they awoke Him and said to Him, "Teacher, do You not care that we are perishing?" ³⁹Then He arose and rebuked the wind, and said to the sea, "Peace, be still!" And the wind ceased and there was a great calm. ⁴⁰But

83

Why Us?

He said to them, "Why are you so fearful?
How is it that you have no faith?" [41]And
they feared exceedingly, and said to one
another, "Who can this be, that even the
wind and the sea obey Him!"

Even the disciples needed to see God's power. He allowed the storm, but when they reached out to him, He answered. He calmed the storm. Those disciples would always have that day to look back on. When doubt crept in, they could say, "Remember that time when we were dying at sea? Jesus commanded the storm to stop." And it did. Even the disciples who were alive with Jesus, who listened to his teaching first-hand, needed to experience His work in their lives. There is no doubt, this changed their lives.

God has used these events in my life to strengthen my faith. He has changed my life. I would have never considered writing a book before this. These things have given me new insight into the trials of others. He has given me opportunities to be there for others. I have been able to minister to others. I have been able to provide comfort to others struggling with medical issues.

It is amazing how God has led me on this journey. A few months after we came home from the hospital with Luke, I felt like God was telling me to write down what happened. After avoiding this for a while, I started to write down some of the details. As spring turned into summer, I felt the urging to share a testimony at church of how God worked in these situations in our lives. I ignored this for a while. Pastor even suggested to me that I share the story sometime. I tried to ignore that too. Every week the sermon seemed to be telling me to share the story. I finally gave in and asked Pastor if we could schedule it. The next week, a good friend at church asked me how I was doing. He said, "You look like someone has removed a ton of bricks off your back. You look so much better than you have recently. Things must be going better." I was amazed at the difference when I quit fighting what God wanted me to do.

I felt like God has been dropping hints to me about writing a book. It started in the hospital. One of the doctors made a comment about it. Since then several others have been telling my wife and me that we should write a book. For a long time, I assumed that meant Anji should write a book.

In October, Anji and I went away for the weekend. We went to a conference about Finishing Well and Leaving an Intentional Legacy. We had both decided independently that we didn't want to talk to others there about "Our Story". We didn't share this decision with each other until after the weekend was over.

Throughout the weekend, person after person would ask us detailed questions that led us to share. One person said, "Tell me about your oldest child." It seemed like they just kept asking until we started to share the story. Then they would encourage us to share more. Then they would tell us, "You need to share your story."

One day at lunch we sat at a table with one of the speakers, and he kept asking probing questions. I finally shared the story with him and he thanked me for sharing it. That night, after he was done speaking, I had him sign the copy of his book that I had. He told me that, while he was sharing his talk, all he could think of was the story I shared with him. He told me, "You have to share your story."

In the next couple of weeks, it became very evident that God was telling me that I needed to write a book. It didn't take me as long this time to listen. I started to pray about what He wanted me to share. I started to take notes when I felt like He was telling me something. Before long, I had a list of chapters.

Shortly thereafter, I was out of town for work. I had been praying for guidance about what to write. I woke up about 5:00 AM in my hotel room. I couldn't get back to sleep. I grabbed my phone and opened my daily devotions. I try to make devotions the first thing I read every day. It talked about writing and sharing God's story. I immediately pulled out my laptop and started writing. Before I needed to get in the shower, Chapter 1 was done. And I felt better. I shared my devotions with Anji that morning. I told her that I was feeling led to write. She wasn't completely surprised. I think we both felt bombarded with people telling us that we should do it.

I got up early the next Monday morning. Before work, I started to research about how to write a book and get it published. The things I found seemed hard and expensive. I decided that I was not going to let that detour me. I didn't share any of this with Anji. Around midnight that same day, Anji forwarded me an email. It was titled, "How To Fearlessly Write An Amazing Book." It was for a webinar titled, "How To Fearlessly Write An Amazing Book In 90 Days That Builds Your Confidence, Grows Your Income, And Leaves A Legacy." When I read this the next morning, I signed up and attended the webinar. I received a free eBook for attending, called "Book Launch." I read the whole thing that night. I decided that writing a book was definitely something I could do.

The following weekend I asked Anji to go away with me for a night. I had been traveling a lot and we had not had time to connect. While we were away, I shared with her details about the book. She wasn't as surprised as I thought she would be. I shared with her the chapter headings. She said, "You are serious about this." She was immediately supportive. I had been very careful not to share with anyone until I had a few chapters written. I didn't want anyone to squash my desire to write. After I shared with Anji, we met with two couples who were good friends. We asked them to pray for us and the book.

Faith shared a quote with me. There is some debate about where it came from. Some credit Albert Einstein, though there is no evidence he said it. It is also not consistent with his beliefs. All that said, here is the quote: "There are only two ways to live your life. One is as though nothing is a miracle. The other is as though everything is a miracle." I have chosen to adhere to the last sentence of that quote. God answers prayers. Scripture tells us so. We have witnessed many miracles. Don't be afraid to pray boldly. Then listen. It has amazed me how I see God working in my life when I pay attention. I encourage you to pay attention in your life. See how God is working. When rough days come, and they will, you can look back and remember how God has worked in your life. You can pray with confidence that He will answer.

I want to close with a final thought. Anji and I had this conversation multiple times through all of this. It would start something like this: "How do people make it through life, especially tragedy, without God?" It is amazing the peace God can bring to your life, if you let Him. He doesn't say it is going to be easy. But if you accept Jesus as your Lord and Savior, He will bring you a peace that passes all understanding. His word says so, and I can attest to it from my life. You can rest in the knowledge that He is in control and He has a plan. It is often hard to see what the plan is in the moment. I know without a doubt that he has great plans for Luke. Through a human perspective, he should not be here with us today. His car was destroyed except for the driver's seat area. Medically, the damage to his brain, shown on the MRI, does not match the outcome. Is Luke who he was before the accident? No. None of us are.

I can assure you, God is at work. He is molding us into who He wants us to be. I can tell you that looking back at my life, I am glad I followed God's plan and not mine. Anji and I are closer than ever. We have always had a good marriage; these trials have made it stronger. My relationship with God has never been better.

Luke is still healing. This chapter in our life is not over. God is still at work.

We have witnessed many miracles in this last year and a half. I would be lying if I said I understood God's purpose in all of this. It could be to bring Anji and I closer together, or maybe to deepen my relationship with Him. Maybe there is someone who needed to read this book; maybe all of these. I don't know. This last year and a half has changed how I look at trials. I now see them as an opportunity for God to work in my life. I know that they will make me stronger. God is Good. I know one thing for sure: His scripture says He will use all things for good, so I know He will.

I would like to share one last scripture with you.

Jeremiah 17:7-8

"7Blessed is the man who trusts in the Lord,

90

Why Us?

And whose hope is the Lord.
[8]For he shall be like a tree planted by the
waters,
Which spreads out its roots by the river,
And will not fear when heat comes;
But its leaf will be green,
And will not be anxious in the year of
drought,
Nor will cease from yielding fruit."

Put your trust in the Lord. Follow his leading. Make it a point every day to watch for God at work in your life. When life gets messy, with God's help, you will be ready to weather the storm.

So, I ask you: If you have not invited Jesus Christ into your heart, what are you waiting for?

Takeaway:

- Pray boldly and listen and watch for the answer.

- God will fight for you, if you ask.

- Cover everything in Love and Prayer.

A Word from the Author

I have felt the Lord lead me to write this book. If you enjoyed this book, please help me to share this message with as many people as possible. Consider leaving a review on Amazon. Reviews help people find books that they will enjoy reading. Also tell your friends and family about this book. I appreciate your help in spreading God's word.

Thank You,

Rob Schmersal

Acknowledgments

First and foremost, I would like to thank God. I am so grateful for how He has helped me to grow through these trials. I thank Him for the way He has answered prayers, when He said yes and no. I would also like to thank my wife, Anji. She has stood by me in the good times and bad. Her support was instrumental in making this book become a reality. I would like to thank Betty Berkey for editing this book. I would like to thank our children for their support, prayers, and proofreading. I am grateful to our family and friends who prayed for and supported us through this journey, both the trials and the writing of this book. I would also like to thank my brother-in-law Jim for taking the picture of Luke's car, that is on the front cover of the book. And one last thank you to my launch team, I really appreciate your support.

Made in the USA
Middletown, DE
24 March 2018